Mind the Gaps

Mind the Gaps

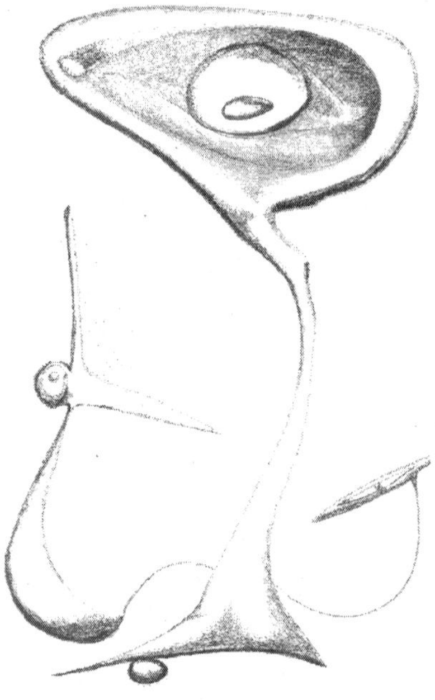

Phil Smith

tp

Published in this first edition in 2026 by:
Triarchy Press
Axminster, UK

www.triarchypress.net

A catalogue record for this book is available from the British Library.

ISBNs:
Print: 978-1-917251-12-9
eBook: 978-1-917251-13-6

Contents

The Gaps

I am writing this because I realise that I have got 'everything' wrong.

By which I don't mean that everything I ever wrote or said has been mistaken. Rather that I have come to think that I have been seriously mistaken about how I have written and thought and spoken about an 'everything', in the sense of any singular totality: forms of society, any general category, the entirety of existence.

I have – and this tracks back for as long as I can remember seriously thinking about anything – misunderstood the relationship between the general and the specific.

What I had never grasped, until just véry recently, is that the nothingness one encounters (maybe in meditation), or the vacuums that appear between objects or events, are not constitutive of some shadowy generality that lies inconsequentially over things; rather they are small, discrete and scattered unevenly throughout the entire cosmos and they drive everything.

It's not that I ever believed it was a good idea to ignore a multiplicity of specificities in favour a singular generality. I never dismissed the specificities. I have often advocated intense attention to details, to the texture of objects, to small and poorly regarded things. I always knew there were lots of gaps around. I long ago heard that story about the physicist who when asked to suggest a reuse for a huge geodesic dome after it was emptied following an Expo, planned to place a tiny ball at the centre while all the rest was kept empty, to represent the correct ratio of mass to vacuum in each atom.

But my big mistake was to assume that it was the generalities, the big structures, the overarching concepts and monster categories that have the important meaning, that are where the power lies, that are the tipping points and the places of leverage. No, it is the gaps.

What if?

What if the universe does not join up everywhere?

There are gaps, most of them very tiny, and they are everywhere. Some of them are enormous. A galaxy wide. Or so densely packed with absence that they can suck a galaxy in. Mostly, we never fall into these big abysses, while the tiny ones are so ubiquitous and miniscule we rarely realise that we should be grateful for walking on so much vacuum without fatally dropping to our doom. Existentially we rely on these gaps.

The universe is positively uneven: if the mass of matter and the mass of anti-matter had been equivalent there would never have been a universe. The two elements would have cancelled each other out. We rely on absences for being. Without an imbalance the cosmos would not have got started.

Which would have been fine. We can be happy about that, and ponder what an incomprehensible magnificence it would have been in its non-existence; more obscure than the most occult secret, darker than the deepest ocean, more desperate than the most hopeless night of the soul, bigger and more voracious than any cosmic monster.

If you just read those last couple of sentences and you did imagine something… anything, no matter how vague and unformed… then there is now a tiny fake nothing-universe within you, a miniscule cosmos of fabricated anti-matter, a non-fragment of the fictional Big Nothing that never was. Nothing much will have happened nor will happen as a result of your imagining, but it is a demonstration of how these little gaps continually pop stuff up out of nothing.

Being is in the imbalance.

Gaps are not necessarily the result of anything going missing; mostly there was never anything there. They are more like the bubbles in a sparkling wine; they are essential to the existence of the whole matter. They are not a question of loss, but the drivers of being.

If That Nothing Is, Then What Is This?

The unevenness and holeyness of space have profound consequences for culture, philosophy and politics. Because – and the conspiracists are right in this respect – things are not how they appear. In everyday life we perceive an unbroken sheet of time across the surface of a world and along which we pass. At a junction one street unproblematically turns into another, beyond a hedge at the edge of one field there is another field, we make an appointment and then meet another person, we follow a river and eventually it falls into the sea. We stand at the estuary of that river and watch the clouds roll in, carrying rain that evaporated from the water in the sea that arrived by the river and will soon be falling again at the river's source, feeding the springs that become its tributaries.

Thinking that such a cycle can be a universal model turns it into a vicious one.

The consequences of the apparent unifying and connecting of all things in a single sheet of mattering have been deadly. They create a strange tension in our feelings and thinking: a dynamic conservatism. Watch a soap opera for a few years and you will see everything happen and nothing change; characters come and go, their names differ, fashions evolve, but their roles and functions conform to the same stereotypical relations. This doesn't matter too much with soap operas, but this idea of a unified dynamic force that conserves a unity in and under everything is what prevails in political economy; that the names and the faces may differ but there will always be some basic structure – hierarchy, food chain, archetype – that like clouds/rain/streams/river/sea prevails, that interconnects everything 'naturally'. So, while it is always possible to tinker here and there with some relation of flows, anything that *obstructs* or *threatens* the flow must be removed (subtly or brutally) to preserve the essential wholeness of the social enterprise. Whether the obstruction be a controversial singer-songwriter, a boatload of refugees or a whole neighbouring people.

Of course, anyone who knows anything about rivers, and the effects when rivers are 'managed' to increase their flow, knows that obstacles, boulders and beavers' damming are not only creative of multiple habitats for varied entities but mitigate erosion and flooding.

But even that, despite its efficacy, is beside the point here!

For the argument here is not that the consistency of generality is less efficient or more anti-ecological than some alternative. This is not an argument about outcomes or effectiveness. The problem for this elevation of all things to the general is that there is no smooth or striated generality by which to hold 'the river'; there is and can never be any one ideal 'river' (or time or social structure or natural process) to which we can ever return or conform; no model through which we can understand and improve each river. Instead, each river has its own model, its own 'ideal' of itself which *every moment* it collapses in favour of a new one or attaches to itself a new one imagined by someone or something else; and all these models are every bit as incomplete and imperfect as the wet things full of twigs, reeds, currents, pools, perch and diaphanous fairy shrimps.

Check out how online 'patriots' use and share the imagery of Britain (often with the help of AI): Spitfires and fish and chips mash up with T-Rexs and eighteen-fingered cricket umpires. There is no 'Britain' that does not have to be invented again today. Inevitably, as always, the idea of it mutates, adopts mistakes, appropriates as 'British' ketchup from India, St George from Turkey, and so on. These are not historical processes, this is ongoing.

When any idea of coherent models is applied to societies or to the cosmos, the problem of rivers pales in significance; for the obstructions are no longer bits of rock but people, communities, entire species. The generality must be allowed to destroy the specificity, as if a generality were ever anything other than a convenient set of clothes worn for a day by specificities; in other words, a generality turns out to be – the opposite of how it seems to itself – a subtraction from the whole.

When a social idea runs up against those obstreperous individuals (or groups) who for whatever reason (self-interest, loyalty to some other model, free-spiritedness, contrariness, prejudice, an experimental psyche, negative associations) cannot be subsumed in the generality, the temptation is to override the nay-sayers – 'for their own good' or for 'the general good' – and start building the prison camps.

While, in each case, the problem and its severity may be directly attributable to one or another quality of the prevailing theory (democratic centralism, eugenics, national security, the *volk*, social justice), the problem begins in the nature of the general categories of theory itself.

Because a whole is not made up *of* a whole but consists mostly of gaps.

What If The Nothing Is A Something?

Humanity, then, has been missing the point, since we stopped seeking out local gods and (post-Ezekiel) began to look to a cosmos-ruling One God.

The attempt to form a coherent cosmogeny or cosmology applied to a unique origin or to the entirety of the meaning of the universe is counter to the nature of the universe that it is seeking to explain. This applies equally to all attempts, whether that be a materialist 'Theory of Everything', an indigenous 'turtles all the way down' or a monotheistic determinism.

Once we have set off down a path to a generality we have become lost in our own dream; we have entered a fragment of the fictional Big Nothing that-never-was that you were invited to dream up at the start of this chapter. At the end of that path, we will be stood in wonder at the centre of a hall of mirrors, believing we see the whole fairground from there.

Where Is If?

William Blake began a poem with the words:

"To see a world in a grain of sand
And a heaven in a wild flower."

To Blake's great credit he wrote of "a world" not "the world", and of "a heaven" not "heaven", for what the poem does is locate the general *within* the specific. The grain and the flower have their own generality; they are not microcosms (which is how the poem is usually read; fitting assumptions to the poem rather than addressing the words actually there). The grain and flower do not hold *the* cosmos in miniature form or dimensionally folded into themselves. Instead, the generality of "world" and "heaven" only have meaning in and as the matter of grains, seeds and petals.

Those like Blake who swim against the tide of generalities are few and far between. To make their sense they often virtuously descend into nonsense and arcane complexity. In some cases, say August Strindberg in his alchemical diary *Inferno*, they ascend and integrate with madness. Extraordinarily, some manage to do both at the same time; think Lewis Carol and Jefferson Airplane's Grace Slick following the White Rabbit.

So 'If' is in the little things. In the trash, in the cast-offs, in banal everyday products.

If, like me, you spend some of your time hanging around the edges of quarries and at the mouths of mines, attending to the spills and overgrown buddles, and to the metallic smell from the streams (still there) – and you should be wary, there may be arsenic in those spills and uranium in those adits – you may feel a presence of something active but absent. I call them 'goblins', but I can just as accurately call them 'ifs'. I can't pretend to have met, spoken with or even seen any of these goblin/if personalities in a solid state, but there is certainly something around these places that is the conflation of labour, tools, processing, potentiality, minerals and subterranean serpent steams. The goblins/ifs are the more-than-human concentrations of the work done there. But they are also the torture of torn rock itself; the ripping and shattering of extracted seams and planetary mantle that persists long after the tools and machines have been put down or turned off; their extracted elements are still running around the world. They are things and events that did not have to happen – there were choices and the falling into routines here – and the potential of not doing them is still present in the ruins of what was done; hence the enchantment.

Holding a piece of coal is meeting an if/goblin. Holding a silver knife is meeting an if/goblin. Finding a piece of plundered Africa is meeting an if/goblin. Every extraction of people and resources has been facilitated by the silver mined under the River Tamar by goblins. Goblins here are goblins there and the goblins there are coming back here.

Question: Are ifs and goblins real?

Answer: in the words of Robert Graves in his poem 'Welsh Incident': "I was coming to that".

You will always be coming to that, when it comes to ifs and goblins. Always coming to them; and they are always coming for you.

Keeping things provisional is important. For we are never entering into a connection or an encounter without some precedent looping up through spacetime to stick itself in our spokes. Sometimes that's a very good thing; if it causes us to fall out of our chariot of gold, or off our high horse. But more often – and the phrase 'to put a spoke in your wheel' has meaning here – the time loop fits too perfectly with contemporarily dominant ideas of authority and the spoke adds itself to the existing cogs in the oppressive machine. Ifs and goblins will be no more helpful to us, despite their provisional natures, than anything else if we seek to make them models for what we do.

Transactions

As with the temptation to do a deal with ifs and goblins, on the basis of a generality, so with certain other kinds of transaction. The temptation within the provisional is to make it a bargaining. 'I will allow this if I get that; I will do that if I get this.'

Small arrangements, mostly harmless. Until there is a crisis; a massive storm, an earthquake that levels a city, an economic crash, crop failure, drought, exile, redundancy or invasion. Then that transactional relationship – 'I sacrifice this, You give me that; I do as You say and I avoid that' – falls apart. Under occupation, in the ruins, in exile (and perhaps this happens at the level of great personal challenge too) we might reflect that we didn't adequately keep our side of the bargain. After all, the generality can't be wrong. But self-criticism is hard (particularly when we are secretly feeling guilty). Much more attractive than confession and correction is the resort, in a time of crisis, to an overarching narrative of apocalyptic transformation wherein our little local trouble turns out to be a small moment of difficulty in the otherwise benign plan of an all-powerful force (a generality) thanks to which we will all eventually be free of our suffering and enslavement. Usually that force is One God, but it can be Nature or some socio-political Ideal; for our mistake was not to have *overestimated* a transactional generality who failed in the face of a landslide or a great flood, but to have *underestimated* a Cosmic Overlord in whose plan the ruin and devastation was all along a crucial part.

Occasionally the 'One God' comes in human form, in the growing pains of Actually Existing Socialism or applies to wrinkles in a market that the liberation of libertarian free will and 'trickle down' economics will surely soon smooth away. For part of the effectiveness of such an Apocalyptic outlook (and it has kept going for well over two millennia now) is to be forever able to put off the final delivery of the Generality's side of the bargain.

Apocalypticism is one-sided transactionalism; the ideological foundation of the dull thrum of anxiety that everyone is encouraged to feel. You *give* everything, the God (state, guru, or whatever) *promises* everything and is always *just about* to deliver.

But never does.

So it is that the super-rich consult leftist futurologists about how to stop their bodyguards executing them when things get 'funky', why firms hire con-artists to teach them how to recognise scams, why comfortably well off but anxious people go into therapy, and why poor people regularly pay a few pounds to an online psychic.

When conceptualised this way the metaphysical swindle is obvious. But that is not how it appears to most people in most everyday lives: no matter how bad things get, no matter how many injustices or 'fuck-ups' they are subjected to, if all these setbacks can be configured as parts of a big plan for Liberation, Transcendence, Good Luck, Elevation, Singularity or Immortality, it is comforting. We put money in the collection plate, we rot in jail, we play the Lottery, we deny ourselves (and others) pleasures in return for the promise of an intangible Ideal. A generality in a hereafter – consoling in the present – that is always moving away from us: in the literature of Apocalypse there is always 'Free Beer Tomorrow'.

It is enormously gratifying, in powerlessness, to be able to imagine that all will turn out well for us (and favoured others) in the end. That our present suffering – even our causing suffering to others – is a sign of how special we will be in the Final Manifestation. A feeling that is endlessly exploitable. Because our immediate experiences, perceptions of the world and sensual potentials are subjugated to and affirmed by an overarching Benign Generality. Thus the tools and matters of a flow of being, a plasmic energy, an *élan vital* are enslaved to the empty categories of an Ideal. With all that wasted energy turned inwards, the common result is the psychic damage of self-punishment, self-disgust, jealousy and the self-righteous persecution of those around us who are insufficiently punishing themselves.

Those who stand in for the One God or the General Idea can inflict suffering as part of their Plan ('this hurts me more than it hurts you') either for their own gratification or to secure their own power; avoiding criticism by invoking the Great Plan which subsumes and validates all their failings and mishaps.

Repentance is *always* a scam; if not for fleecing a congregation then inflicted by the penitent upon themselves. Once a leader has gained acceptance of the idea that their stupidities (winning 125% of a vote, cutting medicine costs by 1000%, stealing from the collection plate, sleeping with prostitutes during the Celibacy Conference, etc.) are parts of a Plan of Redemption, there is little they cannot pass off as a sacrament.

Ends and means are detached from proportionality in the name of evenness and generality: hence the Children's Crusade, the dropping of atom bombs on Hiroshima and Nagasaki, tens of thousands of corrupt 'ministries', the 'Global War On Terror'…

But Wait…

The problem here may be more fundamental than we think. While most (all or almost all?) critiques of the bad things I have referenced above are based on an alternative generality (Marxist critiques of class societies, humanist or materialist critiques of religion, liberal or liberationist critiques of the state, and so on), what if the problem is reproduced by generalities of *any* kind? Of *these* kinds? Which is not to say that every critique based on alternative generality is equivalent to all others in terms of delusions promoted, sufferings caused or degrees of intended malevolence inflicted, but that they are *all* at odds with the cosmos in its immediate presences, in its fundamental particularities and in its gigantic structures.

If that is true, where is The If?

The If is in the cut (or gap) in all matter. It constitutes the space where the quantum realm butts up against the more familiar 'classical' realm; this cut may or may not be an ontological reality. It may be a description of what actually happens in matter; or it may be the best we can do to describe what happens. It was first proposed in discussions about the physicist Neils Bohr's idea of a complementarity in quantum mechanics. According to Bohr's observations, at the quantum scale certain pairs of complementary qualities could never be observed simultaneously; for example, the momentum and position of a quantum particle could not be simultaneously measured. If one quality was accessible to observation the other was not. What Bohr proposed was that it had to be accepted that whatever was going on at the deep quantum level, by its very nature, was always going to be partially mysterious; at the same time 'above' the cut the experimental apparatus capturing information about the mysterious quantum particles could (and should) still be described in classical terms of position, velocity, trajectory and so on. Even though such concepts and descriptions observably made no sense (or made an inadequate sense) below the cut.

Whether epistemological or ontological, the reality of the cut seems hard to dispute. (Is there any difference between Donald Crowhurst *feeling* gravitational waves and him *feeling he felt* them? We'll come to Crowhurst in a few pages.) The cut may not be a place or a thing, but either side of it everything works very differently; no general principles can be applied on one side of the cut and also on the other; yet the cut or gap connects the two realms. On an existential scale the pattern of unevenness prevails and generates becoming.

Imagination, intuition.... don't they work like that? They are not places or things, but they elude definition, they connect things, and they generate stuff that otherwise would not exist.

A Doubt Creeps In

Isn't there a contradiction here? While arguing against generalities, I am repeatedly skipping in this essay from mining to cosmology to religious practices to quantum mechanics to observations on everyday life. And does that not imply – at least in my outlook – some commonality (and therefore generality) that connects, if not unites, these different modes and things? To which I have two responses, which are not necessarily compatible. The first is that such a contradiction in my description is the necessary quality of any description of an uneven cosmos; that an even and internally consistent argument, based on what is there to be observed, will never be possible. The second is that, without falling into an overarching generality, the different modes of things and behaviours described here are parts of numerous webs and networks that connect across categories – hence the possibility for comparisons – without them ever having to constitute a Grand Oneness of Connection. In other words, the 'leap of faith' necessary to jump from one mode to another, or from one thing to another thing, is not a product of faith, but a material requirement of the gaps and 'cuts' between things.

Is Hyper-empiricism The Answer?

The intangibility of the General might seem to point us towards some kind of hyper-empiricism. Ignore the structure, ignore the relations. Ignore the generalities. Go one grain of sand at a time. You never get to know the beach, but, hey, you were never going to anyway.

Sadly, this doesn't work with our 'broken' cosmos.

For there is no fundamental atom, element or indivisible sub-atomic particle to which to turn. At the quantum level the universe is essentially unstable; crossing 'the cut' we cannot rely on empirical data, for it is always partial; falling differently one way from the other. Atomism might be desirable, but there is no reliable 'atom' beyond the atomic and across 'the cut' upon which to rely.

Philosophically, there is some help for us here, in the "swerve" of Lucretius championed as "kinetic materialism" by Thomas Nail. The idea is that matter changes ("swerves" all the time); but the change is not within anything, the swerve is not something that matter does in relation to something else like a context. The change (or swerve) is what matter is.

Also, in the philosophy and practice of Charles Fort.

For Fort believed that it was in the anomalies rather than in any confirming data that reality was to be found. He long ago (1932) grasped the dynamic principle argued for here that there is "nothing, in religion, science or philosophy that is more than the proper thing to wear, for a while" (*Wild Talents*). That rather than what scientists could establish as real, by repeating experiments and getting the same results (or close enough), it was best found in the data that didn't fit, in the gap left within that "close enough" data rather than in its mostly fitting with what had already been agreed was reality.

I think we can go a little further than Fort, however, and say that all the data is anomalous. Even what appears to fit is a construct of the means of measurement. The ways of measuring create the illusion of measuring. And our daily experience – and our hard-wired capacity to edit out what doesn't fit the instrumentalist flow – tells us that such evenness is predictable and reliable and true.

This editing that works for ideological compliance is comparable to how optic flow works for safe transit. When we walk in the street, we don't consciously address each specific obstacle that may fall in our way or every unevenness in the surface; our brain processes the street view in very general terms and 99% of the time that is adequate enough to steer us safely through. (Not much good if we are asked to recall details of passersby, for example.) This is highly selective perception based on assumptions (all the stuff that scientific method proposes to not be). Yet, in science we also get through by approximations. Percentages. Statistics (the low probability that confirmational results could occur by chance). Which is fine in the pragmatics of pedestrianism and science, but less so when it comes to the horrors of eugenic cosmogonies, social cosmologies and religions. Then we need intuition and reverence for anomaly to push away the finding of generalities.

Fort is similarly exemplary in his practices. His wandering into the margins of communications, in newspaper cuttings, in snippets of stories of stories of stories. His speculations on the wild talents of all sorts of agents. His deductions from unreliably sourced data. The exemplary unevenness of his methods and his reluctance to formulate his ideas into anything other than intellectual waystations and lifebuoys is requisite in a universe of gaps. For we are not only "born astride a grave" (as Samuel Beckett would have it) but we live astride one too. Just as Guy Debord, Michelle Bernstein and other members of the 'Situationist International' despised the idea that there could be such a thing as 'situationism', and Karl Marx denied being a Marxist, so I suspect Charles Fort would have been equally alienated by the idea of 'Forteanism'; even 'Forteana' might have given him pause. For if the only predictable thing is the ubiquity of anomalies, any general category or 'ism' is a deception, a deflection from virtuous (that is, somewhat unreliable) examples.

So, is this to favour some version of pragmatism? Or even opportunism? No, it doesn't favour any 'ism'. It doesn't favour any consistency. Nor amoralism. We don't have to subscribe to any particular moral codification in order to avoid violence to, or exploitation of, others – on a personal or a state level. We can arrive at that virtuous doing and thinking by doing and thinking; picking up guidance in bits; we can make our ethics one dilemma at a time and then scrap them until the next quandary; forgetting nothing; attending to consequences and learning from others (saints and monsters and everyone in between). Adherence to a generality has never been a guarantee of anything like care…

Dark Cities

In Alex Proyas's 1998 movie *Dark City*, every night at midnight in a city that is in perpetual darkness, a group of men, the 'Strangers', move the city's architecture around by a collective process they call 'tuning'. On waking the residents adapt their memories to fit with the new shape of the city.

That is how everything occurs in everyday life, without any need for a conspiratorial elite of manipulators. We adapt to all the subtle changes (and even most of the extreme ones) in the world as if they did not happen, as if the world is always the same from one day to the next. We invent the past to be a continuity with the present. Changes that are acknowledged tend to be within the bounds of expectations; excessive ones take a little longer to be accepted into our world view and forgotten or for our world view to be sufficiently massaged.

Understanding that the world is not fixed but is punctuated throughout by tiny quantum vacuums each with the potential to produce unexpected fluctuations helps prepare us for a reality that is all the time swerving, a reality that consists of swerves. The only difference from *Dark City* is that the cosmos doesn't need to wait until midnight every day.

In our personal and individual lives, we can follow the cosmic example: each time we approach a problem, a decision, a project or challenge, we can dismantle our world view, abandoning any totalities or theories we hold dear – including our manners of thinking – and reconfigure ourselves in relation to the specificities of what is before us. Even if we are undertaking a 'kind of' task with which we are familiar and well-practised (mending an engine, hanging wallpaper, writing a poem, whatever) we can say to ourselves, unnerved, "how does anybody do this?" Not to copy anyone else, but in creative incomprehension at how any response might be possible. Through panic and mess the craft can then begin to kick in, appropriate to the bubbles of possibility, rather than mis-matching with yesterday's order.

If that feels too anarchic and chaotic to be practical, temper the moment with a question: "what could possibly go wrong? What's the worst thing that can happen?" Compromising one's innovation when circumstances are predictably hazardous – these bubbles work by probability, for heaven's sake – is far from shameful. Just never assume any probability is inevitable.

How did I get here?

A terrible mistake, I would call it. I have for as long as I can remember tried to form some general picture, some overarching theory, for whatever I have been involved it. Or observed from afar. Often this has been helpful in connecting one aspect of a thing to some other aspect. It has occasionally revealed certain things – motives, plans, organisations, conspiracies even – driving a situation or a movement. But recently it led me into a dangerous place.

I was trying to summarise my thoughts about the ongoing war in Europe following Russia's invasion of Ukraine. Given my understanding of present-day Russia as an attempt to reinstate the apocalyptic authoritarianism of the Soviet Union under symbols of both 'communism' and Tsarism, I regard any success it might have as deeply reactionary; so much of what is being rebuilt there is what we (or, rather, Russians) need to be rid of. In response to the threatened withdrawal of military support by the US Trump government, I found myself arguing for governments in Western Europe to be ready to take the US's place in supplying Ukraine, necessitating an increase in those countries' military spending. Because I felt an obligation to think over an entire situation as if it were a single entity, to which I had a responsibility to think everything through, I ended up advocating something that I was opposed to. Indeed, one word of criticism from one person pulled me up short and I was shocked by what I had written.

I don't think my mistake was simply to wander into militarism. That was bad enough.

It was my attempt to think across an entire situation that upended my judgement; that engendered a sense of obligation to own the consequences of each insight and provide solutions, but without being able to control any of the conditions. It made me wonder whether many of us, particularly when in situations where we have to make decisions that affect others, can be drawn to unhelpful conclusions by our feeling the need for an all-embracing conclusion and action (despite our lacking control of the context). To have a benign Plan that will redeem all eventually, rather than working one small element at a time, aware of how it is connected to other elements by the gaps between them, but working *as if* it were not; in other words by *fictioning*. By imagining the power of the particular; *fictioning* its breaking out of context into autonomy in an 'as if'.

Fictioning is the "writing, imaging, performing or other material instantiation of worlds or social bodies that mark out trajectories different to those engendered by the dominant organisations of life currently in existence" (David Burrows and Simon O'Sullivan). In other words, working in the cuts and gaps of fiction – by intuition and imaginative creativity – to project an otherly non-thing forward in time, one flimsy fiction at a time.

If we try to smooth over the absences, weaknesses, vulnerabilities, cracks and abysses, our concessions to what is there and our impositions on what is not there tend to the authoritarian.

The Empty Temple

To change our mind structure, to let in the gaps, we therefore maybe need to be particularly attentive to certain sacred architectures as examples, at least initially, of *fictioning*. And now as examples of mind maps.

In the Christian and Islamic traditions, people are familiar with the idea of churches or mosques full of people; there for private prayer, study or congregating for religious services. However, the interior of a classical Greek temple would rarely if ever have been visited; maybe a priest might have the annual duty of cleaning the interior. Mostly the temple was left for the god. So that the god could be present, humans needed not to be. There was something sacred about such emptiness.

Since God died in the Western materialist tradition almost two centuries ago, a new opportunity for emptiness has been available. Not much practised, though. Secularists and pagan-revivalists have been keen to refill the empty space of religion with new cosmological certainties; there are any number of scientists who have made their name by secular and rationalist means who have since been keen to tack on some part of Christian theology (or similar) to ward off the emptiness of a materialist belief. Christian revivalists have attempted to shout down the silence with the noisy urgency of apocalypticism.

But what if we embrace such emptiness as an opportunity?

To say "I am nothing".

To sit in the emptiness, and the quietness, and wait.

Or better still, to leave it empty and see what happens close by.

A-causation

A pair of concrete owls stand guard by the chimney stack
Overseeing a herring gull nest; not every outcome
Is the one intended. Or needs to be. A blue sky now; no light was red last night.

Local Generalities

At this halfway point in the essay, it is maybe time to consider some of the ideas here through an extended example: a personal venture that quite accidentally brought its protagonist into an encounter with many of the ideas here. This is the story of the voyage of the *Teignmouth Electron* made in 1968-9.

A few days prior to writing this section, I had set off on the train to the seaside town of Teignmouth. I had wanted to visit a particular church and to sit there for a while, if I was there alone. I leaned against the main door to the church and looked out at the waters beyond the sea wall. I was stood where the sailor Donald Crowhurst was photographed the day before setting off on his fatal 'round the world' voyage on *Teignmouth Electron*. I leaned against the stone frame and was surprised when many grains fell from the sandstone. I wondered if Crowhurst had done the same thing and been as surprised as I was at the dissolving of the solid stone.

Crowhurst was a late entrant to the 'Sunday Times Golden Globe Race'. He was drawn to it, in part, by the large prizes that offered a potential solution to his ailing business and family finances; he was an inexperienced sailor, but he was able to attract some sponsorship, including that from an entrepreneur and from within the town of Teignmouth driven by the town's publicity officer.

The 'Electron' part of his boat's name indicates Donald Crowhurst's technological enthusiasms. (When he stood as a candidate for a local council seat his campaign literature was printed in the style of a computer readout.) He believed that what he lacked in experience at sea might be compensated for by the various technologies he was installing on his boat. Wires ran from all sorts of navigational and sensory devices about the boat to a computer below deck.

The problem was that Crowhurst never managed to build the computer. So, all the wires simply ran to a space where the computer was to have been; a gap surrounded by wire endings.

As he prepared to leave the port at Teignmouth, Crowhurst's lack of preparedness became obvious to those around him. On departure his sails tangled and he had to return to port to get them sorted and start again. Yet he knew he owed a debt of loyalty to all those who had invested in him; Teignmouth was struggling around this time to maintain itself as a tourist destination with desperate 'gimmicks' such as topless waitresses. More to the point, Crowhurst had signed a contract with his main sponsor according to which he would lose his family's home in the event of backing out. He was not in a position to choose; only once out on the ocean, alone with his craft, could he reconfigure himself. Tragically, as he sailed south through the Atlantic, *Teignmouth Electron* began to ship water and it became clear to Crowhurst that it was not sufficiently seaworthy to withstand the Southern Ocean. He held back; with no wish to destroy himself, he sailed in circles, and he began to radio in false accounts of his journey towards the Cape of Good Hope and the Indian Ocean. According to these fake reports he was covering remarkable distances and his feats made headline news in British media.

While all the time Crowhurst was tootling about in mid-Atlantic, inventing reality for an entrepreneur, a publicist and a hungry press, he was reading Einstein's *Relativity: the General and the Special Theory*. After a while he assumed that the other sailors would have overtaken him on their return to the UK, so he set sail for Teignmouth, only to discover that due to mishaps and the decision by one competitor to abandon the race and sail around the world a second time he was in danger of completing the journey in the fastest time; his financial problems would be (briefly) solved, but his existential problems would intensify. Any scrutiny of his logbooks, likely if he won, would reveal damning inconsistencies. He would be humiliated. He would go from hero to cheat in a day.

Crowhurst had invented a fantastical narrative for himself and the UK media had broadcast it to the world. He was one kind of person in the media and a completely other being on *Teignmouth Electron*. Long before the Internet and satellite and cable TV, alone on his boat, Crowhurst felt the 'mass' of a mass media bearing down upon him; how it had been metamorphosing the few gnomic phrases he had been transmitting into a vast idol ready for tearing down. He began to believe that he could directly feel the effects of relativity. He had messed with time and space in his reports and invented a new spacetime in which he was a heroic figure; in the same way that the curvature of space determined the movement of objects, so the distortions in the media he had helped to create were now moving and shaping him and drawing him towards disaster. In place of the missing computer, he had inserted himself into the gap; connected to everything by radio waves, media, gravitational ripples and tendril-wires, he was both a god and nothing.

Donald Crowhurst, in his diary entries, was anticipating a future in which humans would manipulate spacetime and displace God; a singularity in which all ties (wires) with matter would be cut. He had, in anticipation, he thought, become a 'cosmic being' and whereas deception was commonplace for humans, having dispensed in his new cosmic identity with the duality of good and evil in favour of a unifying truth, to deceive was truly terrifying to him. The curvature of the gap had drawn him into its swerve. Picking up the boat's chronometer, Donald Crowhurst stepped off the boat. His last diary entry read: "It is finished. It is finished. IT IS THE MERCY." And then he added a few more words in which he tried again to reconcile his 'cosmic being' with what he had done and was about to do. Leaving in the middle of a sentence….

Teignmouth Electron was found drifting and towed to the Caribbean where it was sold to a New York choreographer as a pleasure boat. Passing through various hands, it was eventually abandoned on Cayman Brac, one of the smaller

Cayman Islands, where it continues to rot away, stripped of all fitments and equipment by souvenir hunters, among the trees at the back of a beach. A gap.

I had gone to Teignmouth to contemplate Crowhurst's existential dilemma. To sit in the emptiness of the large church of St Michael, where Crowhurst had refused to be photographed praying; hence the photo of him at the church door. I eschewed the nave and sat in the Mary chapel. I was alone in the vast space of the church. I settled, I quietened, I wondered. I looked to my left and the archway between this chapel and the chancel perfectly framed a statue of St Michael stood by the altar; and I walked though to examine it more closely.

It was very dark. I could barely make out the details. St Michael held a very thin tubular spear with which he had impaled the crusty reptilian shape of the Devil. The Evil One looked like a piece of excrement. The angel's face was conventionally austere, somewhat blank. In the stained-glass window above the altar, a bright red and orange flame burned through the top of the angel's head. He wore a red St George cross over his armour.

I considered angels.

They are terrifying. Not for nothing do they announce themselves with the words "Fear not!" They are no friends to humans, having voted for us not to exist. In Merkabah Mysticism they form a guard preventing humans from reaching the throne of God, only circumvented, by those willing to risk death, madness and heresy, by self-purification, code-words and deft manoeuvres within celestial palaces. They fill with prohibitions and obstacles the gaps in which we might meet a god.

Yet, this is not how angels are generally portrayed; which is saintly, only military when slaying the Evil One. Often, they are sentimental Christmas Card figures, or New Age guardian 'good luck' charmers. In church art they are often paradoxical. When portrayed in combat with the Devil, the angel towering over the Opposite of God, I like to take their photograph and invert it. It is strange to note how often the two figures of Archangel and Archdemon are pleasingly balanced; they make a satisfying pattern; they are interwoven by the shaft of the spear and the curl of the serpentine tail. The cruel dualism of good/evil and spirit/matter is subverted by art. Because any halfway decent artist tends to a localised generality, rather than an overarching cliché, integrating the beast/dragon/serpent/Opposer with the Positive; the Negative with the Angel. Rather than a supernatural militiaman the Angel in art is a connector, an electrician, a technician, a maintenance man keeping communications open.

All the might of the institutions – the repetition of their creeds and liturgies day after day week after week, year in and year out – is necessary to keep these localised generalities contained within the paradox of a Big Generality. The contradiction is evident in any Christian church that has not succumbed to the self-cannibalising logic of Protestantism. Other religions practice varying degrees of aniconism, or are periodically wracked by spasms of iconoclasm, attempting to avoid the dilemma that Donald Crowhurst took on himself alone, that accompanies every mention or appearance of angels and demons, that bedevils theologies, mysticisms and materialist cosmologies: what to do with the gaps?

The Ghost

What if Crowhurst had not died, but had arrived back at Teignmouth and chosen truth over defending his actions?

If he had challenged the media and the money that forced him to continue to sail when he knew his boat would never survive the voyage? If he had chosen to say, “I became something else on *Teignmouth Electron*; I am no longer human. I am a cosmic being. I felt the effects of curvature in spacetime; they are a greater power than either media or money, and media and money do everything they can to keep from everyone what scientists have known for over half a century: that nothing is as it appears.”

Is his ghost, the cosmic being that he thought he was but could not become, the model for us?

CMB and The Occult Origin

What if Donald Crowhurst was not deluded? What if he really *did* experience relativity? What if he *felt* gravitational waves?

Or maybe he just *felt he felt* them? If so, is there any difference? How would you tell? Doesn't feeling, subjective understanding, the phenomenology of embodied experience trump all else in such a situation? All our science is founded on observation; no matter how mechanised or digitised at some point a human interpreter is required to make sense of the data and communicate the findings.

Maybe Crowhurst stepped off the boat less because he feared the shame of being called a cheat or a madman and more because he feared the responsibility of conveying to entire 'civilisations' their millennia-old mistake?

Yet science was on Crowhurst's side. Consider how every moment a series of microwaves, what scientists call Cosmic Microwave Background (or CMB), ripples through our bodies. These are (according to those scientists' interpretations) the vibrations from the Big Bang, spreading outwards almost immediately after the universe came into being. These ripples now expand out from everywhere in the cosmos because the universe was so small when it came into being, so its 'centre' is now everywhere. There are tiny (but measurable) variations in these microwaves – for the cosmos was uneven from the start – and if we map these variations in the CMB (and scientists have) against the sky they broadly follow the giant concentrations of matter in the cosmos. In other words, an imprecise but meaningful map of the universe is constantly passing through our bodies. Every body in the universe (whether human, rock, insect, water molecule or moon) is thus cartographically connected by CMB to every other body in the universe. Every thing in the cosmos is a localised generality of the entire cosmos.

BUT there is a gap.

Because the ripples – like all the other information we have about the Big Bang – only tell us something about the state of the cosmos a few nano-seconds *after* it comes into being. And NOTHING about *before* or at the point of initiation. Maybe the universe is a product of another universe collapsing (a Big Bang following a Big Crunch)? Or maybe it is made up of matter sucked into a Black Hole and spat out the other side in super-concentrated form? Or maybe some Higher Being concocted it in some other reality? Or maybe it is the work of space fairies? Maybe anything… because there is an event horizon just after the universe's origin beyond which we cannot 'see', because such was the density of its mass and energy that no evidence has escaped it.

So, the origin of the universe is – and looks like it may always be – an occult one.

Based on which seemingly hard and fast rule, in a universe in which there are no hard and fast rules, are we willing to accept two things?

One: that generalities are only ever localised.

Two: that gaps (hidden, occult nothings) are essential parts of what is.

No, three things!

Three: that attempting to fill the gap of the occult with some big generality like a cosmic God, or Nihilism or Rationalism, or Gaia or Pan or even Empiricism, is to traduce the cosmos's essential quality of Occult Mystery.

In other words, to repeat the discovery of mystics and initiated holy ones throughout the ages that having gained access – by ordeals, pilgrimages, sacrifices, purifications, codes and passwords – to the Holy of Holies, there is Nothing there. That the Occult Mystery was always hidden and yet available everywhere along the way, present in its unknowability at each stage of the ceremony, in each stone or puddle on the pilgrim's way. That what is truly hidden will remain hidden.

The One Tear That Isn't There

It is time to consider an exception. For a celebration of understanding based on anomalies, it doesn't pay to spend too much time on consistencies. For while culture has been all about the suppression of its gaps, there is one particular rip in the fabric that culture has been very keen to enforce over and again. That is the gap between the natural and the supernatural. Even those who do not believe in a 'supernatural' often still believe in the gap.

But what if there isn't one?

What if a thing either exists or it doesn't?

Let's take ghosts. My least favourite 'supernatural'. If there is something there – the energy left by a person who is no longer alive, a trapped soul, a messenger from 'beyond the grave' – then there is some *thing* there. If we see it then it is either reflecting or emitting light. Light is made up of photons. Photons have no mass, but they are real. They have energy. They are a part of nature. You don't need supernature for an apparition.

We don't need to have a realm beyond or separate from nature to have ghosts.

And that applies to any other thing that is described as 'supernatural'. The category is superfluous. If the ghost, demon, spirit, portal, vision of angels or whatever is real, then it is a part of nature. In the same way that humans are part of nature. We need to take anomalies like visions and ghosts and humans back into nature; otherwise we will never understand how to be parts of an ecology.

The Seal

I have attempted above to show how cuts and gaps cohere with contemporary physics, draw occult mystery into a respectable cosmology, integrate ghosts with nature, and help us to understand matters that are bitty and holey, but they are also applicable to everyday experiences.

There is a particular stretch of beach that I like to walk occasionally. It is a rather tedious stretch. There is a striking red cliff at the back of the beach, and a railway line, but the sand itself is flat, the beach is partly pebbles; there are few if any landmarks, rarely any driftwood, no groynes to mark it into sections. On a day when the sea is calm, I like to walk along and watch the water. Almost always there is nothing but the soft undulations of the green-grey surface; then the other day a seal's head popped up, had a look around, disappeared again, and did not reappear.

The emptiness of the temple is like that. It is a 'quantum vacuum', having no mass or energy of its own, but every now and then, it will borrow some zip from somewhere hidden and something will briefly pop into being, reveal itself and promptly disappear. Leaving no trace. No explanation, no cosmogeny, no message, no evidence; just a brief flash of something temporarily there.

Within the gap, on the tedious stretch of a wearing footpath on a hot day, or alone in an empty temple, these revelations do not come often or predictably. They are unlikely to be significant in themselves but serve as reminders that the nothingness to which we attend is not an absence but a potent vacuum, a gap with meaning, a meaningful meaninglessness, an abyss with portents, a dark stage that only ever briefly brightens before falling back into motionless.

We can search out such empty temples in caves, in deserted factories, in rarely visited naves, uninviting underpasses, between the rusty pillars beneath seaside piers, in redundant quarries, empty theatres and cinemas, in shopping arcades after closing time; these are all places to stop and contemplate nothingness and attend to any momentary pops of absurdist being there.

Next time you are on a ridge above a valley, looking across that vast expanse of space between the hills and down to the valley floor, if you are lucky you may see a pheasant – a bird that is clumsy on the ground – gracefully slide through that mass, encompassing it end to end in a single glide. A temporary and unlikely 'particle' from the vacuum. Once sensitised to the valley and the glide, you will be ready to experience something similar in abject spaces such as a crowded shopping centre, a deserted quarry or ruined city.

Those insubstantial and brief pops are what *everything* is made of. They are the basic material of the entire universe. Indicative that at some moment, any moment, everything might just 'pop up' and vanish; and that that would not 'matter'.

Non-existence is only a problem for the existing and in this circumstance there wouldn't be any.

Once you have accepted that most of yourself (and everything else) is volatile nothingness, concerns about identity are likely to have far less purchase on you.

Yet this is no basis for loneness or loneliness. The importance of the gap means that disconnection is connection. Dissociation is association. Sometimes this can be uncomfortable; for example, for all those uncompromised people who have no connection to colonialism and now, unlikely as it seems, find that they do.

Trying To Make Non-Existence Meaningful

I want to pick up from that reference to colonialism. For while an attention to gaps and 'cuts' has clear subjective, psychological and philosophical effects, inattention to them (and the imposition on them of false meanings) has had wide-reaching socio-political consequences. To attribute meaning to things that have none has been socially and culturally disastrous. To give this its technical term – Apocalypticism – it is the core of the Western spiritual and political traditions. The idea that there is a far better version of now, soon to be available in a complete form, based on the failure and iniquity of its particular parts, that will involve some turmoil, is in every significant historical event that we endure. From world wars to genocides to utopias turning tyrannical, from slavery to the depredation of the environment by extraction in order to create a hyper-technological paradise; behind them all is the imposition of a Generality that is not there. Even in the grey stability of the 1950s and early 1960s in Britain there was the idea, best expressed in the Fabian gradualism of Anthony Crossland, of approaching utopia at 2% per year. Until 1979 everyone in the UK was riding a slow omnibus along a rocket-like arrow of time that was pointing to a better future. Then its terminus was replaced by 'an even better one'.

The social and historical implications are obvious; for such Generalities can never arrive. They do not exist even in possibility; they are never among those somethings that 'pop up' out of a vacuum. Inevitable failure leads either to the punishment of those scapegoats blamed for its non-realisation or the enforcement of a belief in its existence despite all appearances under threat of punishments for apostasy, treason or indecency. At a personal level, every time we identify a problem or expose an injustice, there is an impetus to contextualise that revelation as part of an overarching plan – our own or some Higher Force's – that will begin with righting this wrong and then end with all wrongs firmly put in their place.

Wisdom is to draw on the gap that can help prevent us from leaping from the specific to the All-General; for the tendency of the gaps is to the anti-apocalyptic.

Gaps are cabins in the woods that actually work; because nothing else comes near them without falling for them. And when nothing falls for a gap, you have an imaginary tiny fake Cosmos. (Let's call this art, but we could just as well say dream.)

Despite the depredations apocalypticism has recently wrought on mass democracy – never forgetting that Hitler was initially elected – there is no reason to abandon democracy itself, either as a principle or a practice. Not only because all the alternatives are worse, but because universal suffrage is one of the few mechanisms that has sufficient mass to restrain the concentrations of state and capital. Giving attention to the gaps and cuts and caesuras does not require any extreme behaviour; this is all best done discreetly. Under cover of the humdrum.

In relation to Apocalypticism there is no reason to separate a consideration of the effects on politics from those of its 'spiritual' fallout. For the Apocalyptic tradition, with various tributaries – including Judaism's Merkavah mysticism and the visionary literature of early Christianity – has long turned the spiritual landscape upside down. Where previously an ancient mystic would expect to descend into the Garden of God, risking death, madness and heresy for a chance to see (or even sit on) the throne of God, something over two thousand years ago this became a rising up to a heaven to see the winged and wheeled throne – the chariot – of God. Matter and spirit were divided one from the other. Divinity became a global superiority. There is only space in such a heaven for one cosmological God; but there are many pretenders to the chariot (the weapon of cattle-rustling and war).

Other social-aesthetics are, of course, available – from Wabi-Sabi to Viennese Actionism – but what dominates in the West (and has been Western-imposed or autonomously adopted throughout parts of the rest of the world) is the raising of a dominant Generality as the ideal form and style of a society and a model for all its individuals. In terms of subjectivity this has imposed the necessity for self-improvement or transcendence, which can take any form from a culturally affirmed sexual voracity to breatharianism, from raising one's asking price to increasing one's numbers of Instagram followers, workforce or entourage. Whatever route is chosen there is always 'to be' some final wedding of the short-term sordid scramble (for more lovers, ecstasies, factories, plantations, votes, masses, flags, drugs, terabytes, Euros or whatever) to the Singularity by which the redeemed individual is obliterated by their Ideal and rises above their past, their practice, their craft, their property, their sins and their violence to the higher reality of Fame, Sainthood, Reputation, Honour, Icon or Media Sensation and their disappearance as a body.

Just as first century (CE) Gnostic contempt for materiality manifested in extremes of asceticism and physical self-indulgence (indifferent to the body, either way), so an overriding Generality, while having the appearance of an overarching ethical framework, has actually turned out to be a licence for cruelty in the short and medium term and redemption for the privileged criminals at the end.

A Body Returned

Maybe there are performative equivalents to the volatile possibilities of quantum bubbles; things you can do.

Mine have included dressing in the clothes of a deceased person important to me and burying myself on a beach in a storm; just prior to this, laying myself on two supporting branches of a tree and letting the wind shake me; with a close friend spontaneously taking vertebrae from an entire sheep's skeleton picked clean by crows and threading them onto white and red woollen threads and (without a word said between us) swinging them into a candy cane spiral…

It is hard to know what such actions mean. Even when they are open to interpretation as symbols or driven by a recognisable psychology they do not sit (as far as I know) within any ritual tradition or ceremonial practice. But maybe their spontaneity (rather than any hit or miss symbolic meaning they may or may not hold) speaks something to an uneven cosmos?

To be ready for spontaneity you need, perversely, to be prepared. This is one of the many holes in the arguments here; the vacuums that hold everything together are the rents that break everything apart.

When a space for spontaneity opens up and a bubble unfolds and beckons you in, that is because the gap has volition, agency and personality. But the invitation and welcome won't necessarily be easy ones. At the very least you might need to be carrying something with you to offer in thanks for this invitation – a small piece of metal, a seed, a splinter of wood, a length of string – which may help to appease the generous emptiness when you eventually 'close it down'. For, as with any conventionally magical working, to let it run free into everything is exciting but may fall way beyond your tolerance for loss of control. That's not a wrong thing to do, but it is a risk. At all events, avoid bargaining; just give what you have. So, lengths of wool and paper shapes, pebbles and coins, or whatever you guess you might need (or later have learned you may need) are things to take with you.

At the end of whatever you do, if there is more than one of you, break something (a glass, a stick, a vase) and everyone take a piece of the broken object away. If there are more pieces than people, then place whatever is left over carefully. When you next meet up, try to put the pieces back together from what people bring. What is missing is something for you to 'read something into' and to work with.

When we 'read something into' something, we put it there.

Anti-transactional

The gaps I am writing about here are not comprised of spirit. They are not made of some non-material element such as what people call a 'soul'. They are not zones that have escaped from the material world; they are the fundamental instability of the material world itself. However, we should be very careful not to impose the extractive and transactional processes of human societies on this instability. Not that anything terrible will necessarily happen to us, but more likely because nothing much will change. Things will just carry on as disastrously as usual.

In worst-case scenarios, we will combine transactional relations with high spirituality.

Whatever we do there will be swerve.

Researching Tantra I came across a podcast advocating a 'sex magic' in which the practitioner wished to sell a house for a price and therefore fixated on the desired sum during sex and – lo, and behold! – that's the figure they were offered. Even if we take the story at its face value, the actual magical operation is the opposite of what the practitioner described; rather than gaining money by sex they had turned sex into money. They had put a price tag on themselves and their lover. They had turned a gap, in this case ecstasy, a rare place in which one might be free of transactions, into a transaction.

The objects you use in 'ritual' should, at best, be worthless in a human market. (I collect trash that reminds me of rockets or flying saucers.) In order to engage with quantum instability, it is maybe best to avoid collapsing the swerving wave; sustain the opening and then offer hospitality rather than trade.

Extend a strand of the ecological web, adding something that will 'disappear' into other things.

While your experiences with the gaps may have the excitement of drama, they are unlikely to disrupt sufficiently to be theatrical. At a larger scale, when a community recognises a gap opening – at Midsummer, at Samhain – then a collective theatricality with horses' skulls on sticks, processions, drum beats and songs may be possible. But at the micro-level, which this is mostly about, there is no need for actors, reverence for any stage that appears is quite enough. Behaving like stagehands, moving a few elements around discreetly, is all you need to do.

Coincidences: Connections Without Causes

If there is such a thing as instrumentalist magic, altering reality by acts of will on the part of a magician – in some traditions of working, by binding demons to bring angels to do the bidding of the mage – the relations of causality are clearly malign there. If 'demons' are the Christianisation of formerly local gods or spirits (*genii loci*) then to force them from their *loci* is already an act of violence against them. To risk a connection with angels (whether fortified by unhappily displaced demons or not) is probably the act of a foolish fool rather than a holy one. If they come, they come, but to *command* them? No. You are playing power games with the ultimate agents of power.

What does seem to happen benignly is coincidence. This is where different elements connect in significant ways, but without any evident causality across the gaps between them. In some cases, of course, some unseen causality may subsequently make itself known, but mostly that does not happen and mostly there is no reason to believe that one was ever in operation. Instead, there has been a connection with an occult causality or an occult emptiness across which things reach. In place of evident causality is the active and agentive gap, the quantum vacuum of the abyss within which all sorts of energies are borrowed and returned, often without leaving any traces of their effects or origins.

Bending Time: Cause And Effect

The general everyday assumption is that time moves in a single direction and in a smooth progress from past through present to future.

In fact, it would be far better if we imagined time as a series of lurches, punctuated by interruptions and caesuras. In these gaps, the arrow of time trips itself up on curved spacetime and loops the loop or stutters for a moment before once more lurching forwards.

One can see many examples of this kind of disruption or bending of temporal arrows. It is not necessary to perform complex thought experiments with clocks strapped to the front of trains moving at unlikely speeds or measuring light bending around giant bodies like stars. Observe the financial futures markets in which fiscal 'mages' use huge amounts of other people's money to predict the future prices of commodities and then bet on the likelihood of those prices; their choices then inform those prices. They fix the future now.

The present can also change the past. Some seek to airbrush certain things from history; famously Trotsky from a photograph with Stalin, or the entire history and profit of colonialism from the present wealth of the UK. But it happens in less immediately agentive but more creative ways. Take the character of Julia in George Orwell's novel *Nineteen Eighty-Four*. Although the words concerning Julia in the many reprintings of the novel have not changed significantly since the book was written in 1948 and published in 1949, Julia has changed a great deal. Orwell, we have increasingly learned in recent years, was deeply troubled by female sexuality. While heterosexual, he did not always welcome a woman's desire and wrote as much privately. In *Nineteen Eighty-Four* it is clear that he does not wholly approve of Julia's sexual promiscuity with members of the Inner and Outer Parties, despite it being a rebellious act against Big

Brother and in direct contravention of the teachings of the oppressive Anti-Sex League, of which she is a leading member. In 1949 Orwell could rely on a general misogyny for sympathy for his suggestion that Julia's acts of rebellion are in some way tainted when compared to the 'pure' intellectual rebellion of Winston Smith, in his lonely room crouched over his dissident diary. Winston rejoices at acquiring (from a covert member of the Security Services!) a copy of the 'forbidden' book *The Theory And Practice Of Oligarchical Collectivism* by Immanuel Goldstein which has in fact been written by the authorities and (if you can be bothered to read it in the novel) is a recipe for acquiescence and a pessimistic analysis of the ingrained tendency of humans to inequality and oppression. Today, prejudices are different. Fewer people trust intellectuals over sensualists or body positivists. Julia's rebellion is the equal of Winston's and meets the same terrible conclusion. But, if the novel is about staring at the truth and not blinking, Julia's understanding of what she does is far more realistic and incisive (and maybe in the long run more damaging to Big Brother) than Winston's high-flown delusions.

Nineteen Eighty-Four is not the same book now that it was in 1948 or 1949.

Gap Politics

So how might the ideas in this essay apply to contemporary politics? The end of the twentieth century and the beginning of the twenty-first were dominated by neo-liberalism. That idea has, surprisingly rapidly, fallen apart. Its greatest achievement was what it did to those opposing it (just as Margaret Thatcher knew that her greatest achievement was Tony Blair): it manoeuvred liberals and leftists into defending indefensible patricians and bureaucracies that served themselves rather than the people they said they were serving. In the great void left over by the failure of individualism – with the only models remaining being those for predators, narcissists and criminals – there is now an opportunity to rethink what an individual is. To retake the ground of the subjective for the psychonauts, the creative rebels, for transitory and cosmic beings, for the selfless and the multi-selved.

In the 1970s and 1980s an argument was won: individuals trying to exploit other individuals would through competition create a society in which all individuals would benefit. Everyone would by necessity 'raise their game' to stay in the game. In reality, the game (which was corrupted from the start and further skewed by deregulation) divided the world into a minority of very rich winners (many of whom had begun with a head start in wealth and privilege) and a mass of losers; the game then redeployed the remnants of a meritocratic patriarchy to maintain and exacerbate the division. The effects on individuals were terrible: whether in police cells, dark parks or on private islands, sexual predation was industrialised by anti-social media. 40% of those prosecuted for rioting against refugees in 2024 in the UK had previous convictions for domestic abuse: against whom was not the point, at every level of society the point was nastiness for its own sake. Artists and academics became managers and administrators; they found themselves sacking their colleagues. Responsibility and creativity were turned into privileges that could be monetised or transformed into power and entitlement through the gallery system. The 'rebel cop' model created in fiction by actors like Clint Eastwood became a reality.

Getting something 'done', finishing the job by whatever means (the more brutal the better) became a virtue, whether for an administrator, a burger bar manager or an officer commanding a gamer-turned-artilleryman. Criminality had been encouraged in the 1980s; if something was in the 'black economy' it was a matter for celebration; taxes were not paid and money went straight back into the economy (black or otherwise). If the commodities traded were addictive substances or smuggled goods or young girls' bodies it was unfortunate but the fiscal authorities shrugged (extreme libertarians pushed for paedophilia to be legalised; imbalances of power were welcomed in general even if the extremes were an embarrassment). In the early 1980s, Charlie Richardson (patriarch of the nastiest London gang after the Krays) made a programme for Channel 4 denouncing the London Stock Exchange as the most significant criminal gang in London. Governments successively surrendered power to the fiscal institutions; resources that might have been reinvested in the economy sat in bank vaults or worked to inflate property prices. The economy was no longer 'for' anything very much other than to distract much of the population while a minority salted away a lion's share.

The authorities are not going to prosecute. In the USA (and in the UK the process is similarly slowing down) rich and powerful people can delay trials almost permanently. In the rare cases where there are guilty verdicts, perpetrators delay payment of fines and compensation; the recommendations of public inquiries are rarely if ever read by the public and are rarely implemented, and there is always a presidential pardon.... If we accidentally come into contact with a sincere person in authority, we must be thankful, but not rely on it. Or them. We must rely on ourselves, and any tiny connections around us; love is not a romantic bonus but now a survival necessity.

Even if we are not living in an openly totalitarian society, it is necessary to act as if we are living in the possibility of one. To always be aware of routes of escape, in cafés to sit facing the door, to learn to move through cities like ghosts, through the countryside under cover of trees; in everyday life to practice being unremarkable, in order to be remarkable only to those immediately around us, to write anonymously, to learn the tradecraft of spies not in order to spy, but in order not to be visible, to teach our faces how to be masks and how to take the mask off; social gatherings should be conducted with the discretion and secrecy of gay clubs in the 1950s; celebrate the greyness of public life and the bright lights hidden within our pockets and under our eyelids.

George Orwell's *Nineteen Eighty-Four*, despite its misogyny, remains a relevant and crucial text for us. The post-apocalyptic politics of Big Brother are collectivist and dystopian-utopian, but their darkest elements – an extensive surveillance system run by the vast security services of the state – are little different from those perpetrated on us now by private enterprise tech companies. The levels of surveillance are comparable, particularly the ever presence of screens and the obsession with gaining access to our intimate ways of thinking and feeling (in order to crunch the data and produce more efficient algorithms for turning individuals into available generalities).

Those who fall foul of the tech are (or will be) ostracised and publicly humiliated. Although they rarely know it – for the pain of being hounded is mythic in intensity – there is the chance of a gap within such persecution. For, if a victim can eschew redemption and self-help the space of disgrace can be one to turn into intimate grace. By becoming unmonetisable we can become unapproachable. Disgrace can become a creative haven within the bare landscape of exposure.

The secret life of the individual is still crushed less by threats than by over-exposure. And by the decades-long process of thinning down what an individual is. Neo-liberalism was the destruction of the individual by promoting the individual on condition that actual individuals behaved more like herds. The apogee of neo-liberal individualism today is the gang. The best response is not to alternatively identify, but to 'gapify'; to locate one's selves in empty spaces between things, in gaps that algorithms do not attend to, in nameless ambiguities, along cuts that machines and police forces know nothing about.

Under the second Trump regime in the USA, once the world's poster child for free market individualism, the beginnings of a Big Brother state are in the process of being formed beginning with ICE and a shift towards state capitalism (tariffs, military purchase of corporations, the state surcharging of private companies). Europe is in a state of perpetual war with refugees from wars it participated in. Crises tighten everywhere, but they are different from previous crises. Not only has the old nineteenth-century Hegelian hope of a new synthesis, of a mass proletarian anti-thesis creating the first society run by a class with nothing to gain from class, gone; even the hope in the hope has disappeared. Derrida's 'spectres' of Marx turned out to be fumes from a corpse. The masses have been both defeated and, most importantly, dispersed; all classes have been indiscriminately atomised (even the British Royal Family is incapable of coherence). The gravediggers of capitalism are now the capitalists themselves; 'progress' can finally be declared dead. If there are any revolutions to come, they will be the acts of more-than-human agents.

In the meantime, we live. And do that best by making small politics in the gaps and along the cuts. Not in the grand swirl of apocalyptic social or spiritual movements, but in more modest acts to the side of them. In vacuums that briefly open before closing down again; we protect ourselves. We operate like spies in organisations of one, or in tiny cells with one or two intimate others at most. Connected to no other cells. We can combine, with great discretion, in larger events when necessary; counter-demonstrations against the far-right harassment of refugees, for example. But we should ignore the allure of those seeking to build apocalyptic change from such small acts of resistance. Instead, we should give our energy to supporting further small acts.

If anything reconnects us it will not be human.

We will learn to dance with our eyes, to dream while awake, to dissent discreetly, to plan evidently ineffective acts that make a difference, to educate ourselves in dumb insolence, to disguise ourselves as observed exteriors while in invisible rebellion, to be mysteries.

To leave our poems on buses, arrange sticks and stones on forest paths, to learn how to disguise codes to look like accidents.

To work by *hyperstition* and *ludibria*. (Go and find out.)

In the ever-shrinking spaces of subjectivity, squeezed by invasive algorithms and representational over-exposure, by the overwhelming 24/7 tyranny of mediatised drama, by the shrinking and dispersal of mobile screens, by the withering of personalities… in the gaps that are left we might connect to the softest and tiniest of nano-things.

To gravitational waves, intuiting emotional communications from whatever is beyond the limits of the most proximate cosmos.

To the vast quantum fields that connect each tiny packet of energy exchange across voids and galaxies indiscriminately to every other equivalent packet.

To be us/not us, and I/not I.

To be becoming cosmos.

Practice cosmic being.

The gaps can set us free.

There Is Never Any Conclusion

Try not to repeat my mistake.

This text is only to be taken seriously in its particulars. To find anything in it you will need to tear it apart.

It would be a sad irony if you were to take seriously the overarching argument in this text about specificities and Generalities. Because that argument is one of the Generalities I have repeatedly fallen for; with a bit of luck for the last time. But there is no guarantee.

It is better to be open-minded and think in terms of tendencies that will not settle into any category. Something soft like that.

So feel your way to a way of thinking that allows more-than-human things to think with and through you. To be more written than writer. To put self-expression last and allow expression to undo self. To press your selves like wild flowers between the pages of books and work with a blend of words and fragrancies. Find wisdom in the random; intuit what chance is speaking to you in coincidences across fields of space.

About Phil Smith

Phil Smith is a performance-maker, writer and researcher.

He is the author of numerous books and plays. With visual artist and poet Helen Billinghurst, he is one half of Crab & Bee, co-authoring *Crab & Bee's Matter Of Britain* (Peakrill Press) in 2025 and *The Pattern* (Triarchy Press) in 2020.

With Tony Whitehead, Phil is co-author of the novel *Bonelines* (2020), author of the neo-gothic novellas of *The Silversnake Project* (2023) and of *Living In The Magical Mode* in 2022.

He wrote *Albion's Eco-Eerie: Films And TV Of the Haunted Generations* in 2024 (Temporal Boundary Press) and his *Albion's Atomic-Weird* is due out in 2026.

Since 1980 Phil has been company dramaturg for TNT Theatre (Munich) and is an Honorary Associate Researcher at University of Plymouth. He is currently researching diagrammatical performances with Helen Billinghurst, and together they are writing a book about these for Routledge for publication in 2026.

Also published by Triarchy Press

Goblin Queens and Qualia Knights (2024)

The Silversnake Project (2023)

Living in the Magical Mode (2022)

COVERT: A Handbook (2021)

The Pattern (2020)

Bonelines (2020)

Walking Bodies (2020)

TNT The New Theatre (2020)

She is the Sea (2019)

Guidebook for an Armchair Pilgrimage (2019)

The Architect-Walker (2018)

The MK Myth (2018)

Rethinking Mythogeography (2018)

Walking Stumbling Limping Falling (2017)

Anywhere (2016)

A Footbook of Zombie Walking (2015)

Walking's New Movement (2015)

On Walking (2014)

Alice's Dérives in Devonshire (2014)

Enchanted Things (2014)

Counter-Tourism: The Handbook (2013)

Counter-Tourism: A Pocketbook (2012)

A Sardine Street Box of Tricks (2012)

Mythogeography (2010)